# ARIADNE'S THREADS

# Ariadne's Threads

**Kaaren Kitchell**

TEBOT BACH • HUNTINGTON BEACH • CALIFORNIA • 2021

Front cover art: Sharon M. Carter
Book design by: Russel Davis, Gray Dog Press, Spokane, WA

ISBN-10: 1-939678-78-1
ISBN-13: 978-1-939678-78-2

A Tebot Bach book
Tebot Bach, Welsh for little teapot, is a Nonprofit Public Benefit
Corporation, which sponsors workshops, forums, lectures, and
publications. Tebot Bach books are distributed by Small Press
Distribution.

The Tebot Bach Mission: Advancing literacy, strengthening
community, and transforming life experiences with the power of
poetry through readings, workshops, and publications.

This book is made possible by a generous donation from
Steven R. and Lera B. Smith.

www.tebotbach.org

# Contents

## I  Losing

## II  Finding

# III  Roots (Family)

# I

# Losing

## Ariadne in the Labyrinth

There was nothing in the room except a small heater,
a pile of pencils and butcher paper covering the walls,
no windows, no clothes, nothing at all for amusement
except three days of musing and marking the walls.

A memory would arise. I'd mark it down.
It felt like the Last Judgment. What remains
when you're alone and naked in a white room?
I was 22 but had lived many lives,

mostly of abandonment. Mostly my abandoning.
I was finally in my element, stripped of all
that wasn't essential, every expectation,
every rigid puzzle piece.

Beneath the waters, the spirits were boiling—
fish ready to leap to the sun. They flew
onto the walls, as voices, pictures, plays. Silent
hands passed me meals through a slot in the door.

It might have been day or night. The longer I spent
in silence, the stronger and stranger the images.
The naked mind, tracing its journey
on the wall. I was perfectly content.

## Ambrosia (or Losing It)

Crossing the Atlantic by ship with my sister, Jane,
eye muscles so relaxed my vision returns,

I resist my handsome pursuer, Jean D'Ambrosio,
an older man of 21, delicious as his name.

Two virgins, Jane and I, dash around Paris,
eat Croques Monsieurs, stay in a pension run by nuns.

Christian, the French photographer, follows Jane
everywhere. *Don't give in*, I advise.

Mother flies to Paris with the younger three,
drives us to a chalet in Villars.

I eat chocolate in secret, name my teeth, read *L'Étranger*, *La Nausée*,
feel nauseated & strange—too much tidiness and green.

Jean writes, invites me to Zurich. He'll put me up at a nearby hotel.
Mother says yes—surprise! His apartment balcony is open to the full

moon, narrow bed against the wall, above, a framed image
of John-John Kennedy praying to his father in heaven.

We make love, his face radiant, I lie beside him in awe.
This is the gods' ambrosia, better than chocolate by far.

His tears fall on my face. *I'm sorry, sorry, I'll go to Mass
in the morning, I couldn't resist, though I know sex is wrong.*

Out the window, over the city of Zurich, Christ and Mary fly
from me—the last threads of Christian faith and virginity.

## Sister Angel Cloud Fuck

She paints crucified zebras.

The man she would die for loves many.
   She makes giant white wings,
      swallows Orange Sunshine,
         lies down in her long white dress,
           wearing her wings,
              carves the letter L on her arms.

The room begins to shimmer.
Red ribbons stream from her wrists.
   She changes her mind and screams.

He leaves her under the covers in the house of friendship,
drives a van from Amsterdam through Tangiers
to propose to another.
   She goes too.

He drops her at the base of the mountains of Tibet.
   She offers to be a stranger's mule,
      passes through L.A. customs,
         red engine racing,
           goes to jail.

He flies to her rescue from Tokyo.
   She begs him to marry them both.
He chooses his pregnant wife.
   She considers religion,
      takes a Sufi vow,
         walks behind the man chosen for her,
           who used to prefer men.

She stops painting zebras,
   leaving her wings behind.

# Icarus

*They say he was a whole day falling.*
—Robert Graves

Her architect father hoped
she'd follow his designs; her mother said
she'd make some man a fine wife.

What stays with me is the way she left,
this 24-four-year-old
who looked in her last photo

like Botticelli's Venus,
long hair seaweed-tangled
like a mermaid's.

She was Icarus too, who crashed—
first in the car, later, looking for help
for her urge to die, turned away

by the psychiatrist who said,
*You wouldn't want that on your record,*
*would you?*

In a field by the cliff on Maui—
in sleeping bags—under all those stars,
she talked with her sister,

& finally said, *Close your eyes, I love you, I'll be fine.*
When her sister slept, she ran to the edge,
shedding her clothes.

Stripped of impediment, she flew
as if the wings that worked for her father
would keep her from falling.

But I can't end with the indifferent sea.
She is radiance, falling,
wearing nothing but light,

nothing weighing her down.

# Pyramid Lake Pantoum

Light enters water & drowns.
I am thinking a terrible thing.
He lived in the Firehouse then,
building black pyramids that filled the room.

I am thinking a terrible thing.
A pyramid is a tomb for an African king.
Building black pyramids that filled the room;
*All women are mine*, he says.

A pyramid is a tomb for an African king.
One of his women was 14, fatherless.
*All women are mine*, he says.
One carved an L in her wrist.

One of his women was 14, fatherless.
One of them left for Nepal.
One carved an L in her wrist.
And he slipped into my bed.

One of them left for Nepal.
I belonged to his dearest friend.
And he slipped into my bed.
*Get out of here*, I said.

I belonged to his dearest friend.
I never could tell my beloved.
*Get out of here*, I said.
He followed her to Nepal.

I never could tell my beloved.
The one with the L in her wrist came too
when he followed her to Nepal.
He found & married Rain.

The one with the L in her wrist came too.
Least likely to marry, he was the first.
He found & married Rain.
He fathered three daughters.

The least likely to marry, he was the first.
His second daughter drowned in a shallow stream.
He fathered three daughters.
His first daughter leapt off a cliff by the sea.

The second daughter drowned in a shallow stream.
His third daughter's lover was not to his liking.
The first daughter leapt off a cliff by the sea.
The third daughter's photo is ringed in flowers.

His third daughter's lover was not to his liking:
Light swam in Pyramid Lake and drowned.
The third daughter's photo is ringed in flowers,
on his easel beside his painting of her.

Light swam in Pyramid Lake and drowned.
Tears fall like rain
on his easel beside his painting of her.
The Egyptian king sits in his darkened tomb.

As tears fall like rain
I'm thinking a terrible thing.
The Egyptian king sits in his darkened tomb.
*All women are mine*, he says.

# Kit Fox at The Feet of Marion Davies

All that year you lay in bed
listening for his footfall on gravel.
He'd run off with some other woman again.

She came to visit you in the cottage
on her grounds, your mother making beds
in her mansion.

She was luminous, kind.
What could she give you?
What would help you heal?

*Could she bring your father home?*
You were five years old,
you could picture almost anything.

You wanted a merry-go-round, you said.
When you awakened it was there on the lawn,
as big as your house.

Horses of many colors
shining in the sun
rising and falling to music

as if tossed by waves,
on the blue-green skirt
of the Santa Monica Bay beyond.

She was a starfish,
a mermaid. She was a star.
She gave you the keys to your life.

You got well in a day. Later,
you painted yourself with her:
Kit Fox at the Feet of Marion Davies.

You painted her, legs crossed in platform shoes,
sinuous skirt, sitting beside her turquoise pool,
long fingers curved

around one more glass of wine.
You painted yourself as a kit fox,
close beside her shapely legs

mesmerized by her glamour,
her beauty, but most of all
her dazzling sorcery.

# Aphrodite Tripping

I had brown skin,
brown hair,
a brown crochet bikini
and a necklace of
scored brown beads
he'd made for me
from peyote buttons.

He'd scrape the strychnine off the tops,
mix in a little water,
toss the pulp in the coffee grinder
and shape it into African
beads which he strung together,
hung around my neck.

He left our tiny studio each morning
so I could write. I left
each afternoon so he could paint.
I headed for the beach
where I'd pop the beads off one by one,
and the world shimmered
sensual and surreal.
Men sidled over
to where I lay on the striped towel.
I wanted to look at the waves and clouds,
I wanted to write on the sky,
I wanted to be silent, and kind,
and I was. Sometimes they'd understand,
sometimes they'd be resentful—
who did I think I was
saying I'd rather not talk just now?

Two years later I ran into one
on the deck of the Trident
who remembered me on the beach.
You used to be a ten, he said.
A number? Really, a number?

Such wit! Such rich imagination!
Why not tell a woman,
You're high C.
Or midnight blue.
Or two swans on the Thames?

Punished for saying no at your peak,
punished for being scarlet or violet,
punished for being a woman
inciting desire,
or not.

# The Thrill of Annihilation

### 1.

Lydia was a Black Panther,
didn't believe in capitalist
bullshit. When Ron came home
from long days producing records,
she liked to sit in front of the fire
with a stack of his cash in her lap,
watch the green bills flare red,
then gray, make him scream.

### 2.

Artie liked to do it alone
with the mask strapped on.
Everyone warned him not to,
but he knew how
to make it safe—
kneel at the top of the stairs
so if the gas knocked him out
he'd tumble & the mask would fall.
A friend opened the door,
saw his legs. I hope he was laughing
all the way down.

### 3.

Rene used to say if I ever left
he'd shoot me right
where he loved me.
I packed my house all night,
caught a flight at dawn,
disappeared.
It destroyed him, he said,

but not enough to stop him
threatening the next woman
or the next. Eight years
in prison, he's still plotting
revenge on the one
who put him away, counting
the days
until the thrill of annihilation.

## Blue Town

1
I who was never afraid
as a child learn fear
from him,

live in hiding as far as I can go
from the western edge, Sausalito,
little willow grove.

Coming home in Cambridge, I turn the key
silently, fling the door against the wall
in case he's lurking there.

I huddle at the kitchen table
with my new friends,
Friedrich, Rainer and Lou,

the woman who mirrors my fate—
men stabbing themselves,
threatening her—

the kitchen the only room
where I'm sure no one can see in
from the dark.

2
At the bookstore I scan
through the plate glass
for his black Dodge Ram.

The playwright
whose troupe I danced in,
Berkeley in the '60s,

comes in with books to sell.
He asks if he can stay with me
and bring his wife.

She follows well behind him
as he walks beside me
home to Maple Avenue,

she who was once an artist
and maenad, tamed to Muslim obedience
by her once Dionysian man.

He lectures me on prayer
and giving up poetry
as idolatrous imagery,

and when he goes, tells me
I haven't found god. Neither has he,
I know, by the dark he leaves in his wake.

3
When the Minnesota poet
who sounds like my Norwegian kin,
reads Blake and Rumi to music,

something leaps up in me.
I dance down Harvard Street
at midnight, singing,

first bright moment
in this blue blue town.
A wound-up stranger asks the time.

I smell his intent,
cross and hide in the
nearest doorway

600 seconds.
Passing the abandoned
building, I know.

Screaming splits the night.
*"Fuck it!"* he says and caroms off me
like a billiard ball that just missed the pocket.

I curl against a car,
wonder if the person screaming
is all right.  Don't know

till people have gathered around me,
how great
is the alarm in my throat.

## Sculpting Stone

It was far from town
in a sort of nowhere
guarded by no ones,
men and women expecting
the worst
within the walls and without.

They feel me up
as if I'm a crime about to happen.
I lean into the stream
and blister my lip. Scalding water
disguised as a fountain.
Cruelty everywhere.

He wears no one's best color, orange.
His words carry a jolt into my current
and back to him electric.
Young sex-starved Black men
leer and laugh and jam
the stream between us.

*Niggers*, he mutters, shocking
me, this California hippie
turned Florida redneck ugly.
*They used to mock me sitting Zen,*
he says. *Now I catch them sitting silent,*
*eyes closed, smiles on their miserable faces.*

*Write it down*, I say. *Write it all down.*
*Not these abstract anyonecouldwritethemanywhere*
*pseudo-zen haiku. Tell it*
*through the particular.*
*How could you, freedom-loving as a flame,*
*have come to use that word?*

Something in him that was always terrible
has grown within these grey walls.
Something has been whipped
and pummeled into a more grotesque shape,
hardened into stone.

## Song for The Earth

Driving North
from Santa Fe,
cloud pueblos
shadow the barrancas.
Before me a jagged rosy ship
sails the pale green desert.

I climb the winding road to Los Alamos,
houses perched on the brink of a fall,
streets with hard and glittering names,
      Trinity,
      Diamond,
the coldness of high brilliant mind.

I would be content to drive forever,
September sun warming my arms,
pools rising behind my lids,
sorrow at living
in such a deadly time.

I become the man inside me
who is like the man I love,
moving incessantly
over this earth,
gathering as I drive,
images of her beauty,
her heart-ravishing beauty.

## True Stories

At El Farol on Canyon Road
they watch a long lean one dance
an Irish jig, precise and gay.

He tells of his father failing. One son
sits radiant as a flower, the other comes and goes
like a mammal anxious before the first snow.

*I could be in love with you,*
he says,
*but I'm not.*

She doesn't fit his pattern,
isn't sad or alcoholic,
needs no rescue.

He talks to her, doesn't run away.
What could inspire anguish here
the way her old love did?

For what is love
if not rescue
or drowning in grief?

They return to Plaza Fatima
following remembered song. Farolitos,
notes of warm music line adobe walls.

Around the bonfires
carollers sing "O Little Town,"
and falter,

hardly recall the words
to old songs about savior
and sorrowful woman.

She drives home, music
of "True Stories" shining like ice,
snow falling, diamonds in gold light.

She gathers wood
he has brought,
makes for him a blaze.

## Dos Equis

The milagro heart beats
beneath my pillow, I eat
almond ice cream missing your taste,
drink a glass of Dos Equis,

because you sign your name with one 'X'
and two are better than one. Fragments
of lines come in silence. I worry
that the words will go when you return.

A Navajo poet's bag of treasures
holds bluebird, turquoise, eagle
feathers—a poet had to know
the ways of eagle, shepherd, clouds.

You call from your room in Labrador,
speak quickly before Klaus returns
with the skin of a baby bear
brought back from the Inuit settlement.

You tell me how the old ways have changed,
how you gave them food and ivory-handled
knives and spent the night. In the morning
they asked for money for lodging.

Each night I record the water level
at Glen Canyon Dam for you while you wander
the earth, listen to her heart just as
a doctor would. I hang

the hummingbird feeder today,
read *The Unbearable Lightness of Being*.
Which are we—the light ones who run away,
or the ones of substance who stay?

## Orpheus' Son

Where there is such genius for surface—
your famous photo of Georgia O'Keefe,
    the texture of the pot,
    her long bony fingers—
someone is steering clear of hell.

Your father gallops across the country,
    frantic gnome,
    pickled boy—
perhaps the dancer in Connecticut is available,
though married,
or the wealthy widow in Tucson?

Your mother,
not entirely mad,
spits words at him
when he visits.

Only you
escaped the family pattern.

There is no woman
somewhere in darkness
who won't forgive you.

You are swifter than he.
You don't go near her realm.
Your devotion to surface is perfect.

## When You Go

The hibiscus blossoms
on the right side,
and I know your heart is with me.

I watch a woman in love with two pickpockets,
t.v. cretins at two in the morning
because you don't call.

Two blossoms on one plant,
two eyes in a face,
two birds in a nest—

no, nothing so cosy, so easy to divide—
it is the wing on a bird you sever,
I live but cannot fly.

That first night I saw at once
how it is between you and your soul,
stiff, a bit remote,

though your body was fluid
and close to me, your chair turned
to face me,

as you placed
little chicken wings on my plate,
poured me red wine.

Later I lay with my head
on your chest, felt your heart
sweetness fill the room.

You are earth to me,
in the senses
at home.

Half of my face is shadow
when you go;
one of my wings is still.

## Bad Luck Time

I think of selling the house,
heading south, renting
a whitewashed room above the sea.

I read for two days straight,
going out only for books.

Did you ever fight for a woman?
No, you don't fight.
You drift away, rootless.

I try to picture you feeding
your father in that room
above the mortuary,
mourning doves crying on the roof,
sun impossibly bright
like the winters of my childhood.

You smell the bodies burning.

Three winters now you have chosen leaving
over turning to face me.

Now the gods have turned away, too.
How is it with you?

## Where Wings Would Be

There are two cards on the sill
in this glass tower facing east
where I write & sleep,
collages by a friend of yours,

the winged girl on a rock
prowed like a dark ship—
peering down
at her own reflection?—

no, into depths,
& on the right
the red rose of Eros.
You feel burned you say

as if you were Eros himself
though you've only heard the story once,
leaning over me in bed in the half dark.
You were already packing to go.

I sit up in bed after calling you,
ashamed of saying too much,
hear Psyche say aloud,
*He's poison, poison.*

The masseur's hands on my back
say, this is the place of grief—
the place where wings would be
begins to open & weep.

The man who closes the door
on the woman inside
turns her into a beggar
or a witch.

The woman should leave him alone.

## Die Liebe Der Danae, Santa Fe

Walking arroyos all day,
talking to the spirits.

Tiny house, Tano Road,
on a ridge where a puma could live.

Cobalt jays in the piñons;
magpies tracking the snow.

Barranquillas like galleons
sail the valley below.

Our knees, rivers trembling
down in the Opera House.

He magnetic beside me.
I pull away—he's married.

Zeus descends upon Danae,
lightning sunders the sky.

She, rent, glowing
in his shower of molten gold.

*I tried to say no—I did!*
*But who can resist a god?*

# Multiple Choice

She was the first mother
who didn't want me
to marry her son.
It wasn't personal.

It was just that she knew
what he needed: the splendor
in the mountains, the deep
pool, the rapt incessant attention.

She had the eye of an eagle,
the nose of an eagle;
she reminded me of a bird—
an eagle perhaps,

following him with her eyes.
He was giddy all the time,
drunk with the power of his own
beauty, magnified by her gaze.

He resembled Dionysus
with his black curls, bronze skin,
and mouth that had never
been innocent.

Her husband had been wealthy,
but her son—he *was* the wealth.
When he moved into my house,
she knew the very moment

he'd be sliding down my belly.
Midnight, that's when she'd call.
He'd leap to answer: *Yes, Mother.*
*Okay Mother. I will.*

How does this story end?
A) We married and left the country.
B) She moved in with us.
C) They lived happily ever after, she and her son.

No. None of the above.

# Roman Holiday

*Audrey Hepburn rides a motorbike*
*with Gregory Peck past the Spanish Steps in Rome.*
*Children play in the fountain on stone horses.*

Claudia has a sad and serious air, meets me in the bar
wearing cream pants and red covering her heart and feet,
ferries me all over Rome.

We talk of the man we both had loved,
the handsome one who lived with his mother
and drank and smoked and burned

through her fortune, both of us nearly strong
enough to make him leave her, he
not strong enough to make either of us stay.

Up in her mother's ancient apartment, she sits like a child
on the floor with red leather scrapbooks
of her family, her mother a famous Roman beauty,

father one of the oldest Italian names, photos
of them with aristocrats in Paris and Buenos Aires, photos
of him dancing, dining and posing with luscious babes.

The story is already over, I see—the most dazzling woman on earth
couldn't hold this man. And Claudia's latest love, a dashing younger
playwright, ran off with the patroness she found him in New York.

Of course she's sad—the ending is set in stone
right here in her family history. She hasn't entered the waters beneath the city,
underneath the Umbrian hills where her father gave her a castle of her own,

hasn't gone into the lake of the soul where stories are remembered and remade. Her parents aren't divorced, she says, they simply were never married—her father's pull persuaded the Pope

to annul the vows, making Claudia a bastard
like her Dad. The old bastard's running now,
Nazi ticket, for mayor of Rome.

## Man Living With His Mother

He shows me the fiberglass mold he made
of Audrey Hepburn's arm. *"See how tiny
she was? Put your arm in it! See?
She was only five foot two, & skinny."*

Above the couch his painting of the fallen angel,
a skinhead girl, and standing figures—the Pope,
a rabbi and Malcolm X at the Last Supper
looking down on her broken, bloody wings.

And on the wall behind where his mother
sits facing him, blonde beauties
posed on schooners, tight bodies
arched in nerve-singing tension.

*"Look at this,"* he says, & hands me a rock
the size of a football, found in the Black Hills
five miles down where they pipe in cold air
so the miners' shoes won't catch fire.

It is the palest rose netted in a filagree of gold.
*"Rose quartz,"* he says. *"Real gold."*
I say, "People who know rocks
say rose quartz brings love."

*"Chip off a piece right now!"* his mother says.
*"I want love."* "You have to get out
more," I say. *"No,"* she shakes her head.
*"Santa Monica's too dangerous."*

He hoists the rock on top of his hand,
fingers spread. *"Just wear this
as your ring,"* he says. She laughs
like a love-struck girl.

## Naming Ceremony

An hour outside of Holbrook,
a town called Two Guns.

The soft green red gold of the land.
Adobe ruins open to the elements.

Roger said
my totem spirit was a wolf.

Driving out of Flagstaff,
snow on the peaks behind.

Dreamy blue sky and
angel clouds ahead.

Passing Second Mesa, remember
watching Hopi dances with Dan.

Joseph City ahead.
Twin white smoke stacks

beside a pale green building,
Cholla power plant.

What were they doing the other night?
Lying around listening

to each other's heartbeats;
the kind of thing that can lead to love.

*Turn this Exit Geronimo* sign,
two cows curled in its shade.

The unraveling of love
is like the uncoiling of your own DNA.

Coming up on two horses,
one brown, one white,

red pickup, a carved Indian face
behind the wheel.

A rusted jalopy on the soft green
gold red earth, nothing crowding it.

Navajo 5 miles. Song on the radio,
female voice: *Why won't you talk to me?*

*You never talk to me.*
*Where do we go from here?*

Male voice: *We're going nowhere.*
Thinking about the him in me.

Two brown cows amble past
a small brown hogan.

What is the name of the man in you?
His name is *Seeing into the Soul.*

Entering Indian Reservation,
two trains passing to the right.

What is the name of the woman in you?
Her name is *Looking Out at Beauty*.

Pink rocks near Chee Indian Center:
giant elephant feet.

Tell me the name of the woman in you.
Tell me the name of the man.

## Two Swans

Quail come at dusk,
their plumed heads bobbing
to eat olives fallen from the trees.

Two wooden swans,
necks curved in longing,
float on a table
in this house of light.

I have a task,
but I am out of time
in the place where two swans
drift inside me—

he, the solitary singer
nearly mute from singing alone;
she, sleek in her cloak of feathers.

Brother,
voice of beauty,
lost lover of the green island,
invite me again to sing.

Across all of the seas
and time between us,
come back.

# II

# Finding

# J. D.

Lifting the left side of your mouth,
becoming Elvis.

Nail in your foot at 7.
You said it hurt. She didn't listen.

2 weeks later she gave you a quarter
for a bus to the hospital alone.

You lost everything in the San Francisco fire.
They replaced nothing, used the insurance money

to move up in the world. Marin County,
you were the only kid who was poor.

They made fun of your clothes at school.
You took to breaking and entering.

Her boyfriend came to dinner.
You didn't want ham, you said.

*Make yourself a peanut butter & jelly sandwich,*
she said, and drove you to the library,

never returned.
You lived in foster homes.

You were 12 years old.
She thought she could kill you.

You boys unwanted by your mothers
grow up to be

great lovers
or killers.

I will die
before I leave you.

# Green Roses

Your hand on your chest, you tell me
of the word lodged there, the same one
caught in my throat.

The crown on the building at Pier & Main
reminds me of a wedding cake, & you.

Two dachshunds wag their tails for a bite
of Danish from a young girl in a gold
flowered dress on a bench beside her father.

This sensation in my chest
of weight and lightness at once.

Next to the Novel Cafe they have painted
over the girl on the back of the bull
ringed by roses & doves.

I've never loved a wealthy man,
only men who are rich.

Sparrows are quick to nip
the crumbs beneath chairs.
I buy two green roses for you.

What can a writer do to earn his bread?
This one's young & tan & bald.

He sits on the Venice boardwalk
by the sea weaving palm fronds
into gold & green roses.

You are a man who has traveled to the kingdom
underground, turned your lead into gold.

Come reign in me.

# The Poster of Kali in Your Office

There she was, bloodied
fangs, the corpses on the floor.
I sat on the desk; you moved between my legs.

You would marry me before I met her,
you said, though I never did, you'd cut
her out of your life.

Your father at 17, on their first date, opened
the door to her house. She, from the top of the stairs,
threw a knife at her brother, Bud.

It missed, lodged in the wall
of my heart last night.
What did your father say?

He should have turned
and left the house.
But then I wouldn't have you,

or her, so huge in ours,
I can't find a room
where she doesn't crouch:

in the dining room where I read,
ask you to let me finish a page
before we go upstairs,

but you can't hear me,
only hear her
saying, Go away.

In our bed,
your legs churn all night,
trying to outrun her,

but she's got you
like a nail in the foot,
a knife in the heart.

# Ariadne's Crane Dance: Life With The Minotaur

### Poseidon's Black Thread

I hear the honking
of a flock of geese

### Dionysus' Purple Thread

In our room above the sea on Crete,
wearing only your natural fur
and panama hat

you dance
the Minotaur dance
for me alone.

### Artemis' Pink Thread

Guests in the bedroom,
camped in the living room,
I lie in your arms in the bath,

one candle lighting
the dark, our shadows
leaping the tiles.

### Hermes' Indigo Thread

Because you're the only man I ever met
willing to go as deep or deeper in talk
than I, the last to say *Enough*,

the first to say *Let's take it to someone else,*
*get another point of view,*
we come through.

**Daedalus' Turquoise Thread**

I hear the swift clicking of
your fingers all day on the keys,
the toenails of a hyperactive dog

(though you prefer cats),
the artisan who never stops
even when sleeping.

**Athena's Green Thread**

Our prayer:
to earn our daily bread
from the work of our muses alone.

**Hestia's Yellow Thread**

You help me pack all day,
paintings, silverware, ten years of my life
in Santa Fe. We light a candle in every corner

of the empty house, write
a loving letter to the new owner
who never replies.

Before we leave, you fill the red bird
feeders hanging from the piñon, so many
it shines like a Christmas tree.

## Aphrodite's Goldenrod Thread

We lie on your bed on Paloma Street,
flames rise from the sheets, light
bursting the skin of the room.

## Demeter's Brown Thread

A Taurus, you like to drink and eat
anything with garlic, oatmeal,
Guinness and café crème,

chocolate, tsatsiki, dark meat,
turkey thighs, breasts,
lips, skin, all that

feasting with Aphrodite
whom you've always preferred
to the mother goddess, Mary.

## Ares' Orange Thread

On our honeymoon we travel
to Paris, Siena, Athens, Delphi,
Elounda Beach and Rome.

Drunk on the beauty of Paris,
infuriated by Italy, souls blissful
in Greece, our spiritual home.

## Apollo's Red Thread

At the end of a stone jetty in the Aegean Sea
open to cobalt Greek sky, a ring
of mountains that looks like Arizona,

we stand in the center of a circle
of family and friends who play
the 12 Greek goddesses and gods,

repeat after each our vows.
Every one of them weeps
except for Artemis, my mother;

who preferring beauty to emotion,
tough and dry-eyed, says,
*This should be a film.*

## Zeus' Burgundy Thread

I hear you read your poems
at Midnight Special.
It happens exactly the way the myth says—

ridiculous—Cupid shoots an arrow
into my heart. Bull's eye. I sit there,
a target, stunned and amazed.

# Gift

*(For Richard)*

For some it's sound, for others smell or taste
or touch: the way you say *rue*, the astonishing
complexity of warm fresh bread smells
in Poilâne, summer rain sprinkling my arms;
but always it's some living scene that stops me.

The night we passed the doorway of a narrow shop
on Rue Monge, jetlagged, a little lost,
seeing her head bent over the work table,
red hair piled up like Colette's, doing something fine
with her hands.

We watched in silence, the room too full
of blossoming to take in all at once. Everywhere you looked
it was still life with beauty. She was tying
tiny pink roses with small lavender flowers
and a spray of something white, elegant and wild.

I saw again Vermeer: a woman deep inside
something she loves, the room as beautiful as she.
After a while she looked up and smiled, went back
to her task. We stepped inside. I asked her
in my raggedy French who the bouquet was for.

A couple getting married tomorrow.
We're on our honeymoon, I said.
She gazed up from her work. She was 60 or so,
dark brown eyes like the center of sunflowers,
her face as open as flowers, the faces she looked at all day.

Her name was Violette, born on May Day, she said,
then she plucked a handful of rose buds woven
with baby's breath, tied with a ribbon of silver silk,
and handed it to me. It felt like Aphrodite,
Vermeer and Colette in chorus,

*This marriage will be blessed.*

# After The Catacombs
*(For Richard)*

The French with their flair for arranging oranges and flowers,
have done the same with bones,
the tedium of tibii relieved by rows of pleasing roundness.

When skin, muscle and blood are stripped away—
how lovely the pattern of stitching on the skull—
only bone remains.

The brain—gone.
The sensitive nose—gone.
The taste buds (avocado, eggplant, chocolate, salmon)—gone.

The crack in my heel from honeymoon walking all over Paris—
the medicine you applied, kneeling and cutting the bandage
with your new Swiss army knife to fit the curve of my foot—gone.

The hand that holds small white roses edged with pink and baby's breath
Violette gave me—gone.
The thick shiny hair—gone.

The tears that erupt in a room crackling with Van Goghs—gone.
Your skin with my skin—gone.
This belly full of omelette—gone.

These breasts close against the warmth of your heart—gone.
These ears that hear a bell ring once at half past 12—gone.
The slow soft melting in me like honey being heated—gone.

Breathing in, breathing out, the inner wings that fill with air—gone.
*O god of the labyrinth, who takes everything but bone—give us time.*
*Leave us alone.*

# Journey to Delphi

1.

You maneuver us out of Athens,
senses in a state of alarm
as big men on little motorbikes

cut and weave onto sidewalks,
braiding traffic, the European
death rate highest in Greece.

I navigate,
read street signs aloud,
which out of Athens disappear,

the map entirely in Greek.
Finally in Delphi, hot and on edge,
soothed by the cool marble floors

of the Hermes hotel, honeymoon suite
above the abyss. A carpet of cypress
and olive trees slopes

into the Bay of Itea below.

2.

At 4 a. m., roosters and your snoring
and neighbors moving furniture,
I give up on sleep, open a travel book.

The ancients called Delphi the world's center,
where Zeus released two eagles—one flew east,
the other west, and came back together here—

where Apollo killed the Pythoness,
where pilgrims came
with questions:

*What shall I do?*
*Whom shall I marry?*
*Is now the time for war?*

I dream you and I set out
in separate boats, one east, one west,
and came back together in Delphi.

3.

You bring me coffee
on the terrace, mark the English letters
beside the Greek, of places we're heading.

We stand looking into the
steep drop below, a lone gull
circling above us.

No one told us how high
the cliffs, how steep
the abyss in Delphi.

We sit, talking of the weariness
of weeks of constant travel
without work or going within.

The best life on earth is not enough,
without stopping to reshape
the world in art.

4.

We climb past Apollo's temple—
with its carved maxim, "Know thyself"—
to the stadium at the top,

find a stone grotto for water and shade,
watch a crowd of Greek boys
horsing around with their coach.

The man races a 16-year-old
the length of a football field.
*Crazy Greeks!* you say.

It is middle-of-summer, fiery hot noon.
They tear down the field neck and neck
till the boy pulls ahead of the man.

Women were forbidden to watch
the games. If one snuck in, she was thrown
from a certain rock to certain death.

Descending the steep slope, I hear
the cries of the slain priestess,
think of my mother,

muse silenced by her generation
and time. To have had her gift
for medicine and buried it!

I say to her in silence:
*Mother, you who gave me*
*my love of words,*

*I'll steal the time,*
*go down to the Python's realm,*
*find our voice, and return.*

## Praise

Lying by the pool on Santorini in the sun,
reading Miller's *Colossus of Maroussi*
on a Greece long gone,

I watch a small cream and brown striped
spider sidle up, rubbing his antennae
in glee.

*You are beautiful,* I say.

He leaps onto my canvas bag,
ecstatic at being seen for his true self
by one of the two-footed giants. He's heard tales
of massacres, being dropped without silk rope
from towering heights—even the merciful
carry his kin outdoors
when family & web are inside.

I say again, *you are beautiful,*
softly so the young couple a few chairs down
don't think me crazy talking to myself,
or simply vain.

He hops down onto the open page, turns
slowly in a full circle
clockwise
on all eight legs.

Every living thing
loves praise.

# Marley

Marley with the Van Gogh flames
rising above his eyes,
Marley with two orange sherbet party hats
on his head, & his peach nose
& creamy vanilla fur.

Marley with the ashen paws
from catting around under cars,
who sulks when we pack
to leave town, who trails
a cirrus plume behind.

Marley who jumps on my chest
when you call from the road,
stretches his length from my hips
to my cheek, throat
motor in full throttle;

who drapes himself over
your head when we nestle in bed,
who looks incensed when our heat
comes up, & hustles out of the room.

Who wears a Renaissance ruff,
whose ermine coat rises & falls
as he sleeps all day like a king.

Marley who gazes up at you, sapphire
eyes marble-round as you hold him tight
in a turquoise towel while we speed to the vet's,

Marley who lurks in the dark on the porch
looking up at pleated wings
with slitted murderer's eyes,

who pads from room to room
to be close to us & cries
when we shut the door.

Marley who arches his back when saying
goodnight as we lay him down in his room,
who lies on his throne as we sleep,

paws shading his eyes,
or stretched out upside down,
flies like Superman through dream sky.

## Swan Song (An Alchemical Fairy Tale)

Long ago on the Thames
I lived on the Wanderlust, an old barge,
dove one night into black
water as men in white

glided by, playing Bolero on flutes,
drifting east like the swan I approached
too soon. He lunged at me, his neck long as a snake.
*Not yet*, he hissed, *not yet.*

I floated back to the houseboat, danced
to the Stones in a yellow dress
covered with leaves & wet. Not yet
was a promise years later he kept.

I longed for the vision
found in the depths. I tunneled & dug
for decades. A flower grew from that soil—
twelve-petaled, many-colored.

At the end of diving below, I knew myself & him—
we float on liquid mirrors, sing, fly, fierce
& serene, mated in all ways,
mated always till death.

## Swans

*(For Richard)*

There are seven species of swan,
four in the northern hemisphere, all white,

three in the south, all part or wholly black.
The northern four are:

*whooper, trumpeter, tundra and mute.*
The *mute* is quiet—though when angry it hisses.

The *tundra* nests in the cold, treeless north.
The *whooper* lives in Europe and Asia.

The *trumpeter,* partial to warm air,
is also the largest

and has a voice.
I choose this one as totem.

The males are called *cobs,*
the females *pens.*

They swim with large webbed feet
but also do well on land.

They like cross-country trips
and mated, stay together for life.

Floating, they are question marks
and flying, lightning.

In the *triumph ceremony*, male and female face off,
raise their wings, and loudly call:

*Cob! Pen! Cob! Pen!*
We never tire of each other's names.

## California

There's a certain moment heading
south from Oregon on Highway 5
when I glance to the west and there it is—
hills crouched low, muscled haunches,
tawny-furred, amber-eyed predator
set to pounce on passing deer,
like the massive-wheeled 4x4s
that suddenly bear down on your tail
the minute you cross the border—
no matter how fast you flee
one of them will soon be upon you,
intent, deadly, but beautiful
in their sleek steely wills.
The sweet kindness, softness like rain
of Oregon dwellers is gone. We are passing
from water into fire. We are in the land of cougar,
eyes rimmed in kohl like the women of L.A.,
faces shaped like the heart.

# Wishbone

She stood like a wishbone, open.
She stood like a cowgirl
just slid off her horse.

She stood before me,
turned to you, inches from your nose
& smiled, inviting you to come.

(The invitation was
not for me.)
I wanted to leave

but would not
since that was what
she wished.

You stared her down
unruffled, stepped aside
& took my hand.

You saw through her—
hungry ghost
reaching for shape in your eyes.

# On The Road Ode To Richard

*(For our First Wedding Anniversary)*

Signs mark the Rogue River & Savage
Rapids Dam. I think of Tori, the green
canoe she carried on her tomato-red Mercedes,

how we ran the rapids, talked of lost
men, impossible men
before you:

Nature boy, Minotaur, Ferdinand
in blooming fields, destined for wholeness
by your full moon birth:

April 23rd, the day Barcelonans give books
& roses, the birthday you share
with Shakespeare.

You, who commit to love with full
heart, who goes to any length for blossoming,
any distance to give the gift.

You, who thinks birds are angels
keeping an eye on you
everywhere.

*High wind area—*
*wind comes up*
*the minute I see the sign.*

You, who when you fly arrive exhausted
from holding up the plane, took your dying father,
who once dreamed of painting, to Paris.

*Wild—is it orchid?—*
*by the side of the road, every color,*
*sparse little dabs of paint.*

You whose light goes out
as if god had flicked a switch
each night at ten.

*Metal kachinas, reins in their hands,*
*laced from couple to couple,*
*a long train of spirits.*

You who won't stop
till we untangle the lines
between us.

*Bridge over the freeway,*
*a pair of swallows beneath,*
*their flight lilting like music,*

*the dip & curve of song,*
*lively & rapid*
*as Mozart—ecstatic!*

## Gleneden Beach

Because my love has an eye for
birds, when I walk at Salishan I see
houses as landing pads for gulls, trees
as watch towers for rufous-sided towhees,
see lawns as dinner plates for bobbing robins,
the marsh as soup for mallards who nibble & dip.
Four Canada geese stroll the bank, two couples bonded
by goslings the same age, 14 skittering blond balls of fluff.
As I try to outrun the rain, the Great Blue Heron rises,
neck curved back on itself, long legs trailing behind,
with a strange cry floats to the top of a cedar
where he scans the world, like the angels
disguised as birds who follow my love
wherever he goes and travel now
beside me.

## Voices

It's quarter to two in the morning,
the 4th of July. The mockingbirds
trill cheep churr chip
scold—giddy manic nuts
like me after pumping heart
pumping iron this morning,
a heart to heart with my banker
whose husband asked her
*Don't you have feelings for me?*
& she said, *No,* & he said, *Counseling?*
& she said, *Too late. Get out*
*before you get sick* I say. We shake
on it. And I hug my handsome husband
who has placed two wedding cake couples
at the top of the stairs to welcome me home
from the bank, & I wash my lacy bras
& check my e-mail & a classmate says
it was fine to see me at the boarding school reunion
& I finally settle down to writing seven more pages
stopping only for Ben & Jerry's
with hot fudge & nuts hear Jagger sing
*You'll never make a saint of me*
as if anyone's trying to, feel that rock and roll sex
u-al feeling, look for a scarf like the one
Vanessa wore in *Deja Vu,* thrill at finding
a French maid with fried egg breasts & lace apron postcard
& glancing in the mirror am startled to see a woman
in her '40s since I feel like a mad mockingbird
young & overflowing in her fountain all day writing
break to read *Independence Day*—it's voice I love
wild quirky intimate voice & coming home
a burst of red & purple stars in the night sky

& a passage he's marked in a book on the '60s—
*Everyone remembers the politics,*
*no one writes what it was—avoiding the draft*
*& happiness.* And happiness is laughing aloud
as I write the story of privileged
suffering girls, straitjacketed maniacs,
who finally let loose in the '60s
throw their lady-like virginity to the wind
& go a little cuckoo like the mocking birds
who squeak babble whistle warble
shout laugh sing outside my window
this ecstatic summer night.

# Walking in Sycamore Canyon

The sycamores are petrified lightning
rising from the ground.

Three steady notes, then a single note shoots up,
drops down to trill like a scrabbling in the bush.

A crow in the campground
ferries a carrot in his beak.

Small aircraft cross our path,
dip & soar, dip & soar.

Inches of feathers with serious eyes,
a flash of ruby ruff.

A silver squirrel on a branch,
hands held to agitated teeth.

We from the second world walk & talk
about the third—building a room out back for the gods

where their masks can hang on our walls
(though where we'll get the money, only Athena knows),

while I feel the power of this first world—
its actors, the animals—and my pleasure in the play:

plume atop the quail's head like a Renaissance prince,
yet such a timid voice!

## Her Rings of Saturn

The poet in leopard skin coat dances up to my husband
at the reading, extending her arm. *See? I wore them tonight.*
Eight Bakelite bracelets, amber & sky,
I chose for her—late for her party, searching
the shops nearby, though even after bargaining,
they were more than he thought we should spend.
The box the shopkeeper offered wasn't festive enough.
I asked to buy the cookie tin on the counter, with its gypsy
girl in red & gold & blue; she dumped the cookies,
gave us loops of rayon ribbon in butterscotch & grape—
hem binding from a sewing shop, her sister's bright,
thrifty notion. We slipped the bracelets into the tin, cut out
a paper heart & penned a note of love. He was pleased too,
though as usual we were lavish with money and late.
When she opened the gift, she thanked him.
She still thanks him whenever we see her, only him.
Dear romantic dreamer with excellent taste in men,
intent on believing it was he, secretly loving
you, who chose this bouquet of rings to say
what he cannot reveal in words.

# Hestia

This Spanish house overlooking the waves,
shaped like a nautilus shell.
This house that actor Ronald Colman built.
This house a ship sailing to Avalon.

This house where a young boy, barefoot, crushed grapes
with his grandpa in the garage. This house with Dionysus
in the wine cellar, his leopard skin on the floor.

This house which balanced the scales
of the terrible news of illness.
In this house, we healed.

This house we dreamed into being.
This house where Ariadne circles the labyrinth,
where medicine calmed the Minotaur's roar.

We come home to this house surprised that it's ours.
This house where the lights burn in Daedalus' studio
long past dark. This house that rings with poetry.

This house of celebration.
This house of light where Hestia
holds us in her arms.

## Weaving Stories

I tell the story again at Tango on rue Mouffetard over Malbec and *chorizo a la parilla* with the young French poet and the old American master, and I don't know why.

It's 40 summers since I lived it. The Stones were singing "Time is on My Side." A stranger cut in and danced me out the back door of the hot crowded taverna on Mykonos on the waterfront by the sea and wrapped my fingers around his cock.

I wrenched away, shocked, and fled through the cobbled streets to my whitewashed room.

He followed me on the ferry back to London, to Oxford, to the Wanderlust, my houseboat on the Thames. He followed me down to my bed.

He built a man-sized chess set out of scraps from the junkyard in Iffley Meadow, painted a giant chess board on the barge roof, and played chess with passersby who called out moves from the overhead bridge, while I paced below reading "A Midsummer Night's Dream" aloud, and later during raucous nights of Beatles and Stones, the wine and stories flowed.

He earned two months in prison for entering England without a visa. A tooth knocked out in a fight.

When my school year was over we took the train to Barcelona on our way to bartend and waitress in Ibiza.

I had to call my parents. Big mistake, he said. They arrived from Arizona, locked me in their hotel suite, and worked me over for days.

He knew. He'd warned me. He knocked on their hotel room door. My father wouldn't open.

He called my name, banged and shouted. You see? He's crazy, my father said, and dialed the front desk. A team of muscular Spanish men could barely drag him down the plush stairs.

They won. I left with them for two weeks on the Costa Brava. Returned with them to Arizona, never saw him again. Was struck numb by what I'd done. Was leaden with shame and sorrow all that year.

Studied at the local college and deadened the ache with food. It was never mentioned at home.

I needed to learn how to live. I left to study philosophy at U. C. Berkeley. Plato didn't reveal the secret. But I learned a thing or two in the streets and the commune where I lived. I'd never again obey.

Now you tell a story of love that didn't last, I say, ashamed and baffled as to why I'd told this one.

The Frenchman fell in love at 15. It never moved any further than friendship. Twenty years later when he sees her, a mother now, he's glad he fell in love with a woman who's intelligent and lovely in every way.

The American poet doesn't mention the name of his latest flame. He doesn't need to. We know her. She simply faded away, never told him why.

Such sadness we bring each other. Yet some thread of the tapestry remains, two years, 20 years, 40 years later. All week spiders have appeared—on the back of a booth in a bistro facing Notre Dame, or when I open our bedroom window to Paris sky, see a weaver suspended, trembling between the frame.

## Queen Margot

The French call me *Chère Margot.*
The doors of the *Hotel de Sens*

had grown too narrow
by the time they released me from prison.

At 52, I'd grown stout
and bald, though it hardly mattered,

the declining power of skin balanced
by shapelier soul.

I had blond wigs fashioned
from the locks of my valets' hair,

had the doors of the palace widened.
Though 18 years, it wasn't so bad at Usson.

The jailer in my bed each night;
by day my memoirs

about my lovers,
and prayers to Saint Jacob for release.

I never had illusions about
fairness between women and men.

I "knew love" at age 11,
courtesy of my brother,

the very one who incited the king
to imprison me for "insatiable desire,"

my husband, Henri de Navarre—
the one with 52 mistresses.

Life was full again. I built
a little chateau,

Henri remarried, left me
alone with my 20-year-old Count—

but then the 18-year-old carpenter's son
arrived from Usson.

I returned from church one day,
my head full of songs for Saint Jacob,

when the Count shot my carpenter
before my very eyes.

*Strangle him with my garters!* I cried.
They removed his head. He's the only dead lover

whose bit of heart is missing from the girdle
strung with lockets round my waist.

I moved to the chateau, finished
the garden convent I'd promised Jacob,

hired 14 Augustine fathers to sing
his praises round the clock.

I wrote all the lyrics and music myself. Jacob
was the only one who stayed with me to the end.

# Grenade

*"Things that are distressing to see"*
—*The Pillow Book* by Sei Shōnagon

The look on his mouth
wreathed in berries
a smiling sleepy cat
body turned in his chair
leaning into his teenage daughter
curly-haired, lapping it up

shutting out the mother
bitter look around her mouth
father/husband's two faces—
sensual for the daughter
blank for her mother—
a terrible thing to watch.

As if the mother gave birth
to her own younger self
('*Rarus*,' 'an abortive child,' or 'a womb,'
the womb of the Corn-mother
from which the corn sprang)
or the secret feminine soul of her mate,
and he loves only her young, fresh flesh
or perhaps only himself in her, his own inner girl,
and abandons the soul of his wife.
I try to engage her in talk, about the taste of the cider,
she smiles but cannot rise out of hell.

Kore in the poppy fields
picking the scarlet soporifics,
his chariot drawn by black horses
roaring down the chasm that opens
daughter snatched from mother, *de meter,*
down into his dark kingdom.

She grieves
and the earth is barren;
apples do not grow,
cider doesn't flow.
Pomegranate, *grenade*:
the food of the dead.

Lord of the Underworld
knows only his own desire,
and they are both—
Kore who cries out,
Demeter who rages—
his victims.

The father unfolds his length, leaves
the restaurant, daughter close, they stroll
side by side along the rue Vieille-du-Temple.
Drained, hollow, the mother
can barely rise from her seat
and follows far behind.

I want to cry out.
I want to embrace her.
Who will send a message to Hades?
Who will offer the mother blessing?
Who will deliver the daughter from hell
and make the earth fruitful again?

## Jeu De Paume

Across the road
past the pool and tennis court
in the late summer sun,
sheep stuttering ba-ah-ah-ah,
their curved backs
gilded, flowing with gold—
they look like tennis balls!

It's the classic French story:
an apartment in Paris,
a country estate of warm yellow stone, blue
slate roofs, rustic simplicity, elegant proportions,
two houses and barn centuries old,
bedroom after bedroom, where once the green grounds
held 100 or more guests.

The photos, the furniture
amplify the story our hosts tell:
she with her delicate French beauty
looks like a catch for this
moon-faced Moroccan official;
a broken-eared rocking horse;
portraits of the children young and grown.

Here he is with famous heads of state,
his power enhanced,
her beauty fading,
and now they've divided the property,
he in Paris with his mistress,
she in a remote stone house
where suitors will no longer come.

And we, two American couples
descended from European fishermen
and farmers, Puritans and miners of gold,
we who are merely here in a home exchange,
are pierced by the loneliness of the wife.
We raise our glasses in gratitude
for hearts that are deep and true, as long it lasts.

# III

# Roots
# (Family)

# Remembering Dionysus

Remember when you were lost?
No map,
no protective spirits,
as far as you could see?

When the biological mothering
was done & there were no
artistic or spiritual guides
to lead you to your star?

I remember when I was a sad starfish
drifting on the ocean floor.
When the wolf was upon me, & I was
the wolf & nothing could fill me.

When I was cast out of my family for being
the fire that defied my mother.
When I was a hummingbird
tasting every flash of red.

When I was a maenad
& men wanted to die in my arms.
When I was a frightened deer stalked
to the edge of the continent.

When I was a waterfall raging
over my work.
When I was a storm blasting
idiot lovers.

I remember the years before the muse
became my lover, & you became my mate
and I remember being lost,
last night, again.

## My Mother and I Talk About the Sixties

In that photo the night before my wedding,
your hands are around my neck.
I'm laughing, though I choked
on that hold for years. You wanted to kill me
for leading your other lambs astray.
But it was a time of lions—
I couldn't stop the roaring.

# Traces of Her

*(For Betty Heimark Kitchell on Mother's Day)*

She is everywhere
in this house by the sea,
only the simple sea grass
between house and waves.

The pale pink & gold crab
shells in the sand make me think
of her cautious
hold on emotion—

the only place she sidesteps
rather than surges ahead.

The goods in this house:
dictionary on India paper
big as a window,
an entire shelf of bird books

& everywhere I look
unexpected, particular beauty—
masks of Inuit gods
on the dining room wall,

Chinese red hand towels,
paintings of landscape,
of houses of inlaid mother-of-pearl,
ebony and gold, of woman musing.

Her desk faces the sea
where she watches gray whales
steam north to summer homes,
& seals that play among waves.

She listens to the cries of loons
from the lagoon across the road
& gulls & terns
stir her Nordic soul.

Her Zora Neale Hurston book
beside my bed
mirrors her genius
for marriage.

She is in me too
in my passion for words
& stories, my Viking blood,
my choice of a mate.

She lives in my willingness
to speak up—my inability
not to—when things
need moving forward,

& I never knew how much
her heart is my heart
until she lay, heart exposed,
and I sat straight up,

not moving, tears flowing, four
hours, pictured surgeon's hands
skilled and sure inside her chest,
perfectly repairing the highway

to the heart that joined
my father's heart, for life.

# Ode To My Brother, Jon, On His Fiftieth Birthday

My crimes as a child were these:
calling him *panty boy,*
inciting him with my silver tongue
to beat down bathroom doors
& chase me through the desert
with rattlesnake guts,
& belts with sharp silver buckles.
Every sentence he began
with *What if...?* I echoed,
What if, What if, What if...

His only crime against me was
crushing my hamster under
the bookshelf, but it wasn't his
fault, the shelf was heavy & he held it
up as long as he could.

Anyway, he may have had a certain
resentment against rodents
after his pet rat bit him on the penis.

I could tell you so much about him:
his cactus head with pale yellow cholla spines—
he looked like he'd sprung from the desert—
his ears that stuck straight out
so they called him Dumbo at school,
till our mother had them pinned back
like a boxer dog & he turned into
handsome Jonny.

He was a manic terror:
every fall the teacher called Mother
weeping, *I don't know how
to control him, he's so wild.*
And our mother cried to our father,
she didn't know what to do with him either.
Dad said *Let him go,* so he was free
to roam the desert,
and Mummy mountain,
snare rattlesnakes
& skin them into belts, gallop around

on our donkey, Pokey, the way he later roared through
Phoenix on his Harley delivering the harvest
with his girlfriend, Gretchen, whose skirt was
so short it could have been a cummerbund.

Lone boy among four motley sisters,
he knows more about women
than any man in town.

He talks to everyone, makes friends
with the bagger at the market, the wino
in the alley & all the kids on the block,

the kind of guy who spent his fortieth birthday
visiting the Palo Verde nuclear power plant for fun,

who skydives with the wife of a ground-loving
friend on her February birthday,
since one thing these Aquarians like to do
is pour out of airplanes the way water
free falls out of an urn,

who takes a walk with me in Venice & stops
to peel the bark from a cork tree, saying,
*We should send this to Jane for her sculpture,*
when what he really means is *Wood, wood,*
*I could make something out of this,*

who runs up Camelback Mountain at 4 a.m.,
a mountain goat in the dark,

who calls to tell me his friends have bought
our childhood home—the house on Mohave
our father built— & offered him any fixtures.
His biggest thrill is getting the toilet
on which he dripped blood after his rat nipped him,
installed now in his new family home,

who'd get on a plane to anywhere with ten minutes
notice if anyone he loved needed him,

who taught his son's class at Kiva Elementary
a course on desert lizards, how to grab a chuckwalla
by the tail when its head is down a hole: wait
twenty minutes while it blows up its body
until it relaxes, then you can whip it out
& make a pet of it.

My brother who is always ready to lend a hand,
who is rarely on time because he makes time
for everyone, who hasn't an ounce of fat on his frame.
My brother who makes roses bloom,
who laughs even when others are about
some grim business, who is light on his feet,
who is always moving into light.

## Valley of The Sun

Grief takes you into the valley of the shadow,
and you who have known no death or insanity,
no sorrow or abuse,
are traveling lightly still.

Beloved brother, this
is what I started to say to you,
then shook my head in disbelief.
For what death is worse than divorce?

And what is more insane than an angry mate
you've left who covets you still?
And who is more abusive than a woman
lacking work of her own?

And what could be more sorrowful
than a heart full of love that is stoned,
or a man who wanted ten children,
divided from his only one?

# Revolutionary Poem For My Niece Bayu

*Stay through every revolution of the moon till at last*
*you arrive at the sun.*

You were a child playing
by the edge of the sea.
"Will crabby bite my toes?"
you said.

You will return again
to the house of stone,
iguanas dripping like lava
from the roofs.

Your sailor father
will teach you again
how to ride a manta ray
& beat away the sharks.

The blue-footed boobies by the water
& your grandpa Gus
in his cave in the hills
will tell you their stories again.

And Grandma Lou will be down
at her waterfront hotel
raking in the dough.
And your mother, Jane,

will circle the island
with her sweet presence,
her hand-made gifts,
dreaming of escape.

I, her sister, will arrive
to help with the baby, you,
& bring my lightning truth
& your mother will say

of your father one year later
*It's true, he's a tyrant,*
& return to Arizona with you
where she & I began.

And you & the god of loss
will go on turning.
And I & the goddess of truth
will go on speaking.

And Jane & the mother goddess
will go on weaving.
And your father will sparkle & spin
with the god of play.

And you will learn:
to turn from the god of sorrow
to the sparkling god of play,
& so return

to your lost father, wild island,
the crabs & blue-footed boobies,
the original family
of blessing & play.

*Stay for the revolution of planet and life.*
*They turn and turn, return*
*to where they began.*

# Naming Poem

*For Samuel Farrand Kitchell*

What do you call this thing he has,
this sweet shimmer in the soul?
His mother had it even when she lay
in her white gown, hollow bones,
fed by tubes, her life coming to a close.

One of his daughters has it—
stars sparkling on water,
an open innocent something
that doesn't fight,
but is strong.

He, a well-formed man, and tall,
told me he was a runt,
decided at 10 to have no enemies
the rest of his life so he wouldn't
be crushed.

It's quieter than charm,
and deeper. It's in them
when others aren't around.
Another sister calls it
the happy gene.

My father, grandmother, sister—
the ones who have it hum along
like bees plastered on pollen
or gerber daisies, bright
and open, in bloom.

# Hawk

*For Samuel Farrand Kitchell*
*November 6, 1921 – September 11, 2006*

From his bed, he faces Camelback,
Mummy Mountain to the north.
The powerful man of action cannot move.

9/11, eleven of us gather.
He looks like a hawk: the gentle curve of his nose,
silvery feathers on his head, his fierce strength.

Radiance fills the room. Our adoration
surrounds him. 11 pm, his breath stops,
his death the deep echo of his life.

Next morning a hawk lands in the paloverde
outside the window. He faces
my mother at breakfast.

I and three sisters watch.
He is brown and cream
and gold,

one wing awkward, as if he's just assumed
a new form. Eyes bright, composed,
he picks at the feathers on his breast,

gazes at mother, then swivels his head
and stares north, then south
toward my brother's welcoming home.

Then he lifts over the house to the east,
floats the cobalt air between Camelback and Mummy,
above the valley where he built his home.

Mother has never seen a hawk light
near the house before—
it could be a Swainson's, she says.

In the ancestral book, I read
that his family crest was a hawk, wings
raised, belled and jessed, on a field of blue

within a border of gold. A person who does not fear
to make his approach known
to either friend or foe.

How can you imagine his immense,
benevolent spirit unless you knew him as we did?
Yet we who knew him best did not know

until we saw him in the final room, robed in white,
innocent as a boy, regal as a pharaoh,
and keened as if life itself had fled.

## My Father's Masks

Dark sleeper, eyes slits, cheekbones carving a face like a heart, mouth agog, tip of tongue, thin flames shoot up from dreaming brow.

Lord of the Underworld, a fan of eagle wings above his head, Scorsese eyebrows, nose that curves back into his open mouth, eyes that stare at eternity.

Strange seal—chalky blue face with spotted brow, squinty eyes, African nose & tight little crescent-toothed smile—face in the center of his body nipping a blue fish, he's the man in the moon.

Turquoise monkey with abalone eyes, mouth gaping in awe.

The little thunderbird is all beak & black irises—focused, he knows where he's going.

The green bear bares his pearly teeth.

This one's worried—a bitter pill sticks in his craw, eyes reflect light dim as the moon's.

Beautiful gold-skinned woman marked by flame, stricken by what she's seen.

The wolf is hungry, teeth bared, ears like brick chimneys on the pigs' house he's about to blow down.

Here is a dangerous face—blood red, death black fear. Stay away. Don't get near.

Ha ha ha, hee hee hee, his smile's like a boomerang, mask of glee.

The Asian shaman with the Fu Manchu has eagle feathers laced in his hula skirt hair.

# Harvest Moon, 2010

Has it really been four years since I hung my father's Inuit masks,
a circle of twelve spirits on the living room wall, a month after he died?

His Pilgrim ancestors sailed to Connecticut in 1639, and traded land
near Quinnipiac—now New Haven—with the Menunkatuck tribe.

Robert Kitchell and five other English planters
signed a deed of purchase on the 29th of September, 1639,

with the head of the tribe, the so-called Squaw Sachem,
who signed her name with the mark of a bow and arrow,

giving them all the land between the Kuttawoo and Oiockcommock river
for 12 coates, 12 fathom of Wompom, 12 glasses, 12 payer of shooes,

12 Hatchetts, 12 paire of stockings, 12 Hooes, 4 kettles, 12 knives,
12 hatts, 12 poringers, 12 spoons and 2 English coates.

They called the place Guilford. They lived in peace
with the Menunkatuck, never broke their treaty.

I leave the curtains open. His spirit is traveling still,
may want to see these carved faces once worn in the dance.

Upstairs in my study, I hear Marley crying outside.
But no, there he sits like a loaf of ginger bread on the bed.

I slip outside to the balcony and listen. The cry of a cat—impossible!—
six stories up in the palm. A palm exactly 84, my father's span of life.

The fat Harvest Moon shines on the sea, illuminates the fringe of its fronds,
outlines the creature there—an owl? No owl has ever appeared around here.

Perched there he can see the masks on the living room wall. He can see Marley and me in my study upstairs. Could it be…? *Is it you?* I say.

He calls twice, *Hoo hoo.* Again, *Hoo hoo.*
I send him a silent message: *Signal me with three hoo's if it's you.*

I wait. He calls, *Hoo hoo hoo.*
I raise my arms in a dance of joy, exulting:

*Father of kindness, father of good spirits and hard work,*
*father of blessing, I will keep my secret promise to you.*

# Paris: Vision

*For my mother, Betty Heimark Kitchell*

Two eyes (islands)
gaze out from the Seine:
the eye of judgment,
the eye of dream.

We cross into the left eye,
l'Île Saint-Louis, where
Camille Claudel wrestled lost love
into faithful stone,

where Baudelaire wove
his poems out of smoke,
and André Breton wrote
*Les Champs Magnétiques.*

(Here is the place
on her left eye
that teared up,
preventing her from seeing.)

Here, the Pont Saint-Louis where
police tortured a gypsy for a crime;
her mother cursed the bridge
and it crumbled seven times.

On l'Île de la Cité, the right eye,
tulips bend their heads
over smaller blooms
in the park named for a pope;

past blossoming cherry trees,
through the Portal of the Last Judgment,
we enter Notre-Dame,
where he and I

lit a votive below
the painting of mother and child
and prayed to pagan Demeter
for the health of her eye.

Here is the Hôtel Dieu,
the first hospital in Paris,
where a drag queen stands in the quadrangle
dressed like Snow White.

Ici, the Conciergerie
where Marie Antoinette was locked
before losing her head. (Her judges,
Danton and Robespierre, lost theirs too.)

Voici la Sainte-Chapelle, the king's chapel
where 15 windows blaze with blue,
green, gold, red, mauve light
and stars spangle the ceiling.

Here is where we remember our father's
Four Seasons (blossoms opening,
bees buzzing, horses galloping, snow
falling); tears spangle our cheeks.

Here's the Square du Vert-Galant—
the gay blade, Henri IV,
most beloved king of France
astride his bronze horse.

Willows hang heavy as lashes
in the corner of the eye
where the bateaux mouches
depart, where she rises

from her rolling chair, mourning
seat, descends hundreds of steps,
and we embark, exultant,
under the bridges of ghostly faces

carved into stone,
our boat gliding
toward the tower of iron lace
flooded with light.

We have passed
through death, passed
through suffering,
whole!

# Jane

Below the Paris to Seattle sky bus,
I see a cloud path that seems to lead to Shangri-La,
some impossibly beautiful cloud country only spirits can enter,
and I know she is leaving.

*

Were we close?
Only as close as twins
who do not know where one begins
and the other ends.

Were we close?
Only as close as two fledgling elf owls,
one a little noisier, finding shade in a saguaro
from the Arizona heat.

Were we close?
Only as close as two children of tender natures,
daughters of a Viking mother—
magnificent—but tough.

Were we close?
Close as two girls, one who loved playing with dolls,
the other, with characters in books,
both knowing early which would be a mother.

Were we close?
Close as two swimmers
in red tank suits, passing the baton
in a relay race.

Were we close?
Close as two best friends, 11 and 12,
trying out our first tampons
in the bathroom at midnight.

Were we close?
Close as two Nordic girls
who gravitate to the sea,
boarding school in La Jolla.

Were we close?
Close as two astonished virgins
discovering sex the same summer,
one in Zurich, one in Paris.

Were we close?
Close as a pair of ears
thrilling to Dylan's "All Along the Watch Tower"
and "Lay, Lady, Lay."

Were we close?
Close as Betty's daughters, raving about the best books,
*The Wizard of Oz* to *Mrs. Dalloway*,
*Duino Elegies* to *In Arabian Nights*.

Were we close?
Close as two horses
nickering, galloping wild,
in Berkeley in the '60s.

Were we close?
Close as two artists' models
costumed as the Mad Hatter and the Dormouse
at an art class Tea Party in Kroeber Hall.

Were we close?
Close as two Viking daughters
setting sail for adventures in the '70s
on trimaran and schooner.

Were we close?
When one was in trouble in Ecuador,
she didn't have to say it,
the other leaped to go.

Were we close?
Close as two monks
who value simple food
and silence.

Were we close?
All our lives when the phone rang,
we knew
when it was the other.

Were we close?
Praying for each other to find a worthy mate,
one who'd be there through celebration and suffering,
sailing the long distance with us through the end.

Were we close?
Close as daughters of a splendid father,
fighting for him to finish his life as he wished,
exulting with our family when he returned as a hawk.

Were we close?
Close as two art lovers,
speechless at the Louise Bourgeois show in Paris,
a woman who turned herself inside out in her art.

Were we close?
Close as two stars
in opposite constellations,
the Centaur and the Twins.

Were we close?
Close as a dreamer
dreaming with Jane through the bardos,
through the long journey home.

Were we close?
Close as two stars in the same immensity,
connected to each other and you
through our shining.

\*

Out of thick fog,
two points of a star lit with gold,
or the tail of a fish:
Seattle.

Pine trees, gold light
and water.
Serenity over all.
Roar of the plane descending.

Race to Swedish Hospital
with Jon and Leatrice. Already there:
Betty, Suki, Ann, Greg,
Bayu, Rachel and Liza.

Jane in bed,
eyes closed, struggling for breath,
beautiful as ever. We hold her hands,
stroke her brow. An hour later, she goes.

Were we close? Are we close? Always.

# Chartres

Great winds of the great goddess
whistle around the cathedral.

Inside, the priests have tried to hide
her circuitous path with chairs.

We sweep them aside,
wind through the labyrinth.

Sister, father, walk the eleven circuits with me,
one gone six weeks, the other seven years.

I carry them and the longing
of my daemon as I go,

curve through her four-chambered heart,
drink from the holy grail at her core.

## Message to Jane

Where are you now, Jane?
Have you sailed to the Milky Way?
Do you dwell in the heart of our galaxy,
winking at us from Sagittarius?

Do you know what you are to me?
Can you feel my gratitude?
I see you walking in beauty still
at home in the immensity,

visiting me in dreams.
Today is your birth day
but you are beyond measure,
pouring your light into the eternal flow.

*13 December 2013*

## On Reading a Message on 7-16-16 From a Friend of My Sister, Jane

I had a visitation from Jane last night.
A friend of mine was flying to Madison yesterday
to try to see her dad before he died.

I went to bed thinking about her,
and I remembered how you flew in from Paris
and arrived in Seattle for Jane's last hour.

I thought I was asleep, and then I heard myself say,
"I did it. I waited," and I realized it was Jane
speaking through me, saying she waited for you.

I could feel her inside my body
showing me what it felt like
to be her at that time.

She showed me that it was just like
getting into a challenging yoga pose,
and then settling into it, and even finding comfort in it.

She had to slow her heartbeat
and slow her breathing down as far as she could
and still keep alive.

It was a conscious effort to hold on,
but it wasn't really difficult as she knew she could hold on
if she just focused on slowing

everything in her body to the minimum
and not spend any energy on the drama in the room.
She was aware of your journey and your location.

Then I felt a warm wave flood my heart
as Jane showed me her love for you,
a huge kind of love that had no end,

it was a powerful bond, very deep and old;
full of tenderness, devotion, trust, delight,
all the dimensions of love.

There was never any question for her,
you would be with her when she died.
It was a team effort, your coming together for that moment.

It's morning now and I have a full day ahead,
but I had to get this to you.
Blessings, Liza.

## Three Boats or Losing Jane

After she died,
three boats kept me
from drowning:

the gods,
your love,
this pen.

## Thanks to the publications in which some of these poems first appeared, some in variant forms.

*Blue Town* appeared in issue four of *51%* (1999).

*Gift* appeared in issue nine of *Spillway* (1999).

*After the Catacombs* appeared in the anthology, *Don't Blame the Ugly Mug*, Tebot Bach Press (2011), and in a fine art edition in the Getty Museum's handmade books collection.

*Praise* appeared in volume XI of *Rivertalk* (1999).

*On the Road Ode* appeared in volume two, issue one of *Urban Spaghetti* (1999).

*Gleneden Beach* appeared in issue five of *Crimson Crane* (2003).

*Grenade* appeared in the Winter 2013 issue of *Drunken Boat* (2013).

*My Mother and I Talk about the Sixties* appeared in issue five of *Crimson Crane* (2003).

*Hawk* appeared in the anthology, *Letters to the World: Poems from the WOM-PO Listserve*, Red Hen Press (2008).

# Acknowledgements

*Gratitude for guides*: David St. John, Carolyn Kizer, Carolyn Forché, Chris Abani, Laurel Ann Bogen, Alex and Jane Winslow Eliot, Christian Fennell, Molly Fisk, Sam Hamill, Eloise Klein Healy, Dorianne Laux, Suzanne Lummis, Carol Potter, Tristine Rainer.

*Tausend Dank* to David St. John and his poetry master class in Venice, CA: Richard Beban, Jeanette Clough, Beverly Lafontaine, Jim Natal, Jamie O'Halloran, Jan Wesley.

*Grazie mille* to my fiction and memoir s.t.a.r.s.workshop in Playa del Rey, CA: Diane Sherry Case, Jennifer Genest, Jon Hess, Dawna Kemper, Cassandra Lane, John Truby, Anna Waterhouse.

*Muchas gracias* to Carol Cellucci and her poetry workshop in Santa Fe, NM: Frances Hatfield, Judyth Hill, Janet Holmes, Joan Logghe, Jonelle Maison, Angela Menking.

*Merci beaucoup* to my Paris Writers group: Jade Aleesha, Amanda Bestor-Siegal, Chris Buckley, Janet Skeslian Charles, Sion Dayson, Rachel Kesselman, Emily Monaco, Anna Polonyi, Diane Vadino, Laurel Zuckerman, and Shannon Cain who brought us together.

*Wielkie dzięki* to my Hedgebrook poet sisters, the Pleiades: Carolyn Forché, Connie Braun, Robin Davidson, Susan Landgraf, Lisa Morano, Jacquelyn Pope.

*Diolch yn fawr* to Mifanwy Kaiser, for her immense generosity to the poetry community, and the gift of publication.

*Thank you* to my adored parents, Sam and Betty Kitchell, and to my beloved family.

Above all, gratitude to my late husband, Richard Beban, whose love was my surround and ground.

# About the Author

Kaaren Kitchell's writing life began in Paradise Valley, Arizona, where she won the fourth-grade autobiography contest. The promised prize: a trip to Europe. The delivered prize: a film about the same. She stopped entering contests, but years later, she moved to Paris. Her poems have since appeared in numerous literary journals, various anthologies, and in a fine art manuscript at the Getty Museum. She received an MFA in Creative Writing, Fiction, from Antioch University, LA. She has worked as a performance artist, an artist's model, a tutor for blind high school students, a cook on a schooner, a bookseller in NYC, Cambridge, MA, and Sausalito, CA, and an art dealer. She and her late husband, Richard Beban, taught *Living Mythically*, bringing myth into your daily life, at the C.G. Jung Institute in L.A., at Esalen Institute, and in private workshops in the U.S. and Paris. Their blog of her essays and his photos, *Paris Play*, can be found at www.parisplay.com. She is Fiction Editor and Co-Poetry Editor of *TheScreamOnline*, www.thescreamonline.com. To contact Kaaren Kitchell email to: ariadnesweb@msn.com

TEBOT BACH
A 501 (c) (3) Literary Arts Education Non Profit

THE TEBOT BACH MISSION: advancing literacy, strengthening
community, and transforming life experiences with the power of poetry
through readings, workshops, and publications.

THE TEBOT BACH PROGRAMS
1. A poetry reading and writing workshop series for venues such as homeless
shelters, battered women's shelters, nursing homes, senior citizen daycare
centers, Veterans organizations, hospitals, AIDS hospices, correctional
facilities which serve under-represented populations. Participating poets
include: John Balaban, Brendan Constantine, Megan Doherty, Richard Jones,
Dorianne Laux, M.L. Leibler, Laurence Lieberman, Carol Moldaw, Patricia
Smith, Arthur Sze, Carine Topal, Cecilia Woloch.

2. A poetry reading and writing workshop series for the community Southern
California at large, and for schools K-University. The workshops feature
local, national, and international teaching poets; David St. John, Charles
Webb, Wanda Coleman, Amy Gerstler, Patricia Smith, Holly Prado, Dorothy
Lux, Rebecca Seiferle, Suzanne Lummis, Michael Datcher, B.H. Fairchild,
Cecilia Woloch, Chris Abani, Laurel Ann Bogen, Sam Hamill, David Lehman,
Christopher Buckley, Mark Doty.

3. A publishing component to give local, national, and international poets a
venue for publishing and distribution.

Tebot Bach
Box 7887
Huntington Beach, CA 92615-7887
714-968-0905
www.tebotbach.org